Printed in the United States of America

First Printing, 2015

ISBN 978-1512156515

www.laurajaworski.com
gjmeyer.wix.com/portfolio

Jingle Jingle Little Gnome & Other Children's Poems

by Laura Jaworski
Illustrated by Jerry Meyer

A frog named Albie
Hippity Hopped
On his way to the pond

And as he hopped
He passed a toad
That had a magic wand

The toad said, Albie
Come on over
And I'll grant you a wish

A new canoe
Or lily pad
Or your very favorite dish

So Albie stopped
And thought and thought
And thought and thought some more
But really all this thinking had
Become an awful bore

So thank you, but no thank you
Was how Albie did respond
For all he really wanted
Was a nice dip in the pond.

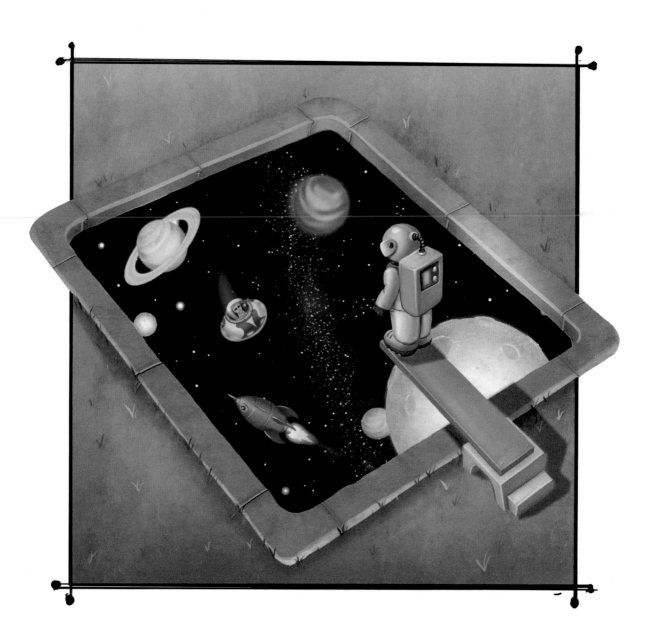

Outer space
Is the perfect place
To go swimming without H_2O

Just make sure you bring
Your cold weather things
'Cause the temp is 500 below!

I am the cupcake caper
The icing caped crusader
And cupcakes unattended
Will soon be apprehended
I'm swift and I am steady
So bakers best be ready
Don't turn around for long...
Or those scrumptious,
Fluffy,
Sugary,
Treats,
Will soon go *poof*
They're gone!

(Yum!)

Two blocks of ice
Feel oh so nice
On chilly penguin feet

Tied nice and tight
To skate all night
Down Penguin Party Street.

Bartholomew the Hippo is a rather funny bloke
He dons his tiki swim trunks while he practices backstrokes
He has a rather festive drink he props up on his tummy
And as he swims his best friend George deals out cards for gin rummy
They chomp on grass for hours and then collect large piles of sticks
So when they've finished eating they can use them as toothpicks
And when Bartholomew is feeling rather bleary-eyed
He opens up his mouth and yawns a yawn
That's three miles wide
Goodnight...

If I had a pirate ship
I'd sail across the seas
With the wind in my hair
Yelling Pirates, beware!
Or your treasure we shall seize!

If I had a pirate ship
I'd sail the ocean blue
With a parrot that talks
And a plank made for walks
And a grubby but fun pirate crew

If I had a pirate ship
I'd adventure the world, round trip!
I'd say Arrr! and Me Hardy!
And have wild pirate parties
If I had a pirate ship!

I'd like to throw a lasso
So high up in the sky
And wrap it round a fluffy cloud
That's slowly floating by

I'll pull pull pull that lasso
Until the cloud comes down
Then hop onto that squishy fluff
And start to roll around

I'll tie my lasso to a tree
And let that white cloud soar!
Then up up up I'll go go go
Like no one has before!

Then high up in the morning sky
I'll close my eyes and smile
While laying on that big white cloud
I think I'll nap a while...

Sweet dreams...

The Traveling Cloud
The Wandering Rain
He goes round the world
Then he goes round again

He's been to Zimbabwe
And to the North Pole
He's traveled to Ankara,
Texas,
And Seoul

Some days he's a vapor
And in constant motion
While others he's droplets
Of rain in the ocean

He's snow when it's chilly
He's rain when it's not
He makes the air moist
When he starts to feel hot

The Traveling Cloud
Oh the places he goes!
And he gets there much faster
When his cousin wind blows!

Family can be...

A mother
A sister
A father
A brother

But, family can also be another...

A friend
A dog
A cat
A bird

Or even an iguana, I have heard!

So with family, really, there's no concealing
It's less of a word, and more of a feeling.

If I had a pet elephant he'd give me rides to school
And we'd wear matching swimming suits while playing in the pool
I'd never have to climb a tree to pick a piece of fruit
He'd lift me on his trunk then let me slide down like a chute

If I had a pet polar bear I'd snuggle in his fur
We'd sled downhill so fast the world would turn into a blur
I'd make a million ice cubes so that he'd stay nice and chilly
And dress him like a coconut when we were feeling silly

If I had a pet monkey we would hang down from the trees
And eat banana bread while swaying lightly in the breeze
He'd teach me how to use my feet just like they were my hands
And make all kinds of jungle calls while practicing headstands

If I had a pet orca whale we'd swim across the ocean
And party with the penguins if we ever had the notion
We'd relay race with dolphins while we swam by passing ships
And snack on lots of ocean treats like salted seaweed chips

If I had all these different pets how happy I would be
But as it is I only have my little pup with me
She's floppy and she's silly and she loves me through and through
So gosh I don't think any other pet (or rather, friend...) would do!

Think happy
Think snappy
Think sparkly & breezy
Think laughy
Think daffy
Think tickled & sneezy
Think brilliant and bold and as bright as the sun
Then take all that happy and go have some fun!

Cheep cheep cheep
Goes the little peep
Moo moo moo
What a hullabaloo!
Cluck cluck cluck
Sounds the alarm
Whatever was I thinking
Moving to a farm!

Frederick Mouse
Lived in a house
In an attic floor three stories high

He had a box on a shelf
That he'd painted himself
And hung curtains because he was shy

He had a neighboring frog
That lived in a log
That paid rent to a toad for a nickel

And each day they'd have coffee
Then share a round toffee
And snack on each end of one pickle

They would slide down the drain
Whenever it rained
And play leapfrog and tag in the yard

They were peas in a pod
And though some found it odd
Being buds for these two wasn't hard

They would laugh every day
In the merriest way
For a true friend can be hard to find

But they'd found each other
Like a frog and mouse brother
And that was the very best kind.

I'm setting up my ladder on a rainbow
To climb the colors to the very top
Can't wait to see the view from on that rainbow
Then slide down to the soft grass with a plop!

A nest would be a lovely place for a nap...

Perched high up in a tree
With a soft and calming breeze
And a little bird asnooze upon my lap.

I am a little wishing well
I'm made of rock and stone
And here upon this little hill
Is where I've made my home

I sit atop the grass so green
And wait for passersby
So they can wish their heart's desires
Or at the very least, can try

For even though I want so much
To grant all their requests
I fear that of their wishes
I will mostly make a mess

A wish for something big will surely
Conjure something small
And if you wish the rain to stop
Expect a massive squall

I am a little wishing well
But till I've had more practice
Don't ask me for a comfy chair
You might sit on a cactus.

There's spaghetti on my head
There's spaghetti on my head
Oh my gosh I think it's spread
Mr. Spaghetti Head

There's a veg ball on my nose
And tomato sauce on my clothes
There's spaghetti on my head
Mr. Spaghetti Head

We were having a family dinner
Mom said whoever finishes first
Is the winner
So my sister took her dinner...

And turned me into
Mr. Spaghetti Head.

Boom
Boom
Back and forth
See the elephants go

Left
Right
In a line
Walking sure and slow

Leading the procession
Marches grandpa, big and strong
The mama and the papa
Follow close and march along

The baby lifts his trunk
And trumpets out a happy call
Then wraps it round his mama's tail
So behind he won't fall

Boom
Boom
Back and forth
See the elephants go

Left
Right
In a line
Walking sure and slow.

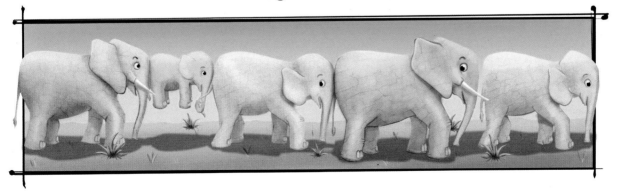

There's a voice
A little voice
That's good and kind and true

There's a light
A little light
That shines inside of you

There's a friend
A lovely friend
That always sees you through

So listen close
'Cause that's your heart
A-whisperin' to you.

Rub a dub a dub a dub
Chicks and ducks are in my tub
Cheep, cheep
Quack, quack
Blub, blub, blub...

How'd a fish get in my tub!?

I'd like a set of cloud shoes
A white and fluffy pair
So I could strap them on my feet
And walk upon the air.

Lamont M. Lareaux
Is a portraiture snail
With a studio in an oak tree

He so loves to paint
That Lamont M. Lareaux
Would be happy to sketch you for free

But Lamont is so slow
That he reaches his tree
Just about when the workday is done

And so it turns out
That Lamont M. Lareaux
Has not painted a portrait, not one!

(Perhaps I will buy him a scooter for his birthday.)

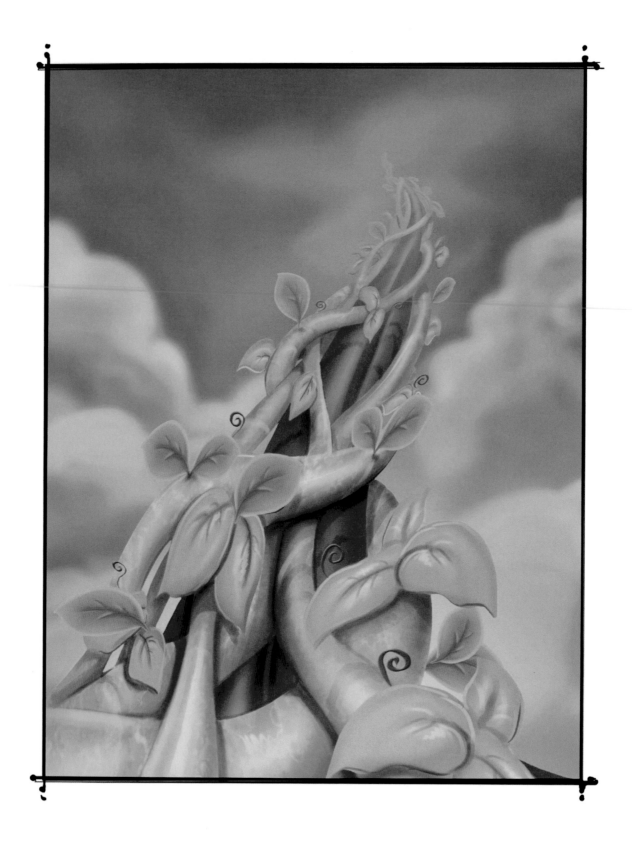

Grow, bean, grow!
Fast, not slow!
And, if you're ever dry...

I'll water, water, water
Maybe more than I ought-er
So you sprout and reach the sky!

There once was a monster named Harry
Who try though he might,
Wasn't scary
For his googly eyes
And their look of surprise
And his soft fur the color of cherries

Just were not scary

Now Harry thought he'd get a teacher
So he found a unique-looking creature
That had eyes that were crossed
And a nose that was lost
And quite misplaced and jumbled-up features

And he just was not scary

So finally Harry decided
That his non-scary self should be prided
So he got up and penned
A short poem for his friend
About how they had been quite misguided

'Cause it's OK not to be scary!

(In other words, you're perfect just the way you are!)

Herm the worm
Squiggles and squirms
As he zips through the garden each day

He goes BOING! through the shrubs
And yells rub a dub dub!
'Cause it feels like the right thing to say

He yells out to the slugs
While he's cutting a rug
'Cause to zoom through the flowers feels great

Then he hides in the dirt
So that he won't get hurt
When he hears someone at the front gate

Herm's best friend is Sherm
Who's a very slow worm
And instead of fast zipping, slow scoots

And when they both feel tired
It's time we retired
Is what Herm says...
As they curl up in a nice piece of fruit

Sweet Dreams!

Splish
Splash
SMACK!
I love to jump outside!

Rumble
Grumble
BOOM!
I think I'd rather hide...

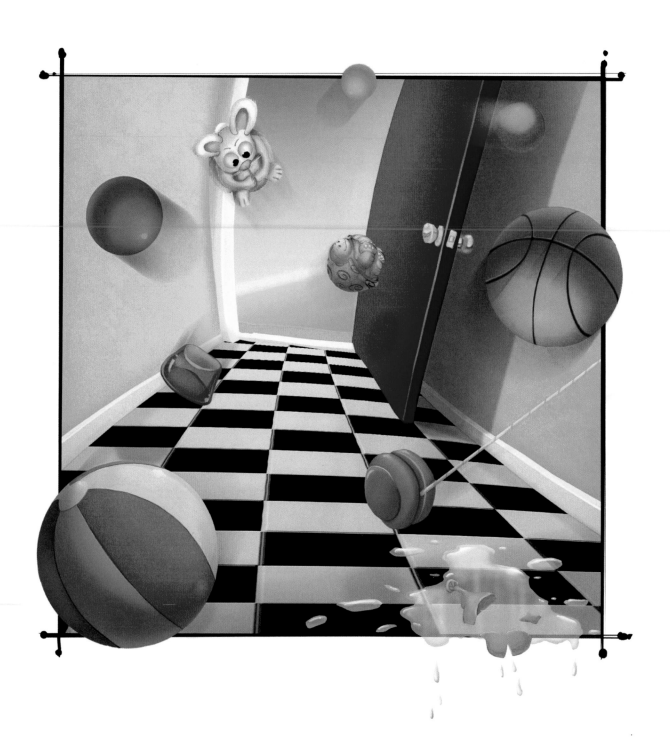

Things That Bounce

I like things that bounce
That bounce and trounce and flounce
I'm always, always boinging things
To see if they will bounce

A rubber ball will bounce
A basketball will bounce
A tennis ball will bounce

Bounce, bounce, bounce!

A furry bunny will bounce
A moon bounce will bounce
Squiggly jelly will bounce

Bounce, bounce, bounce!

A yoyo will bounce
A water balloon will...

Whoops.

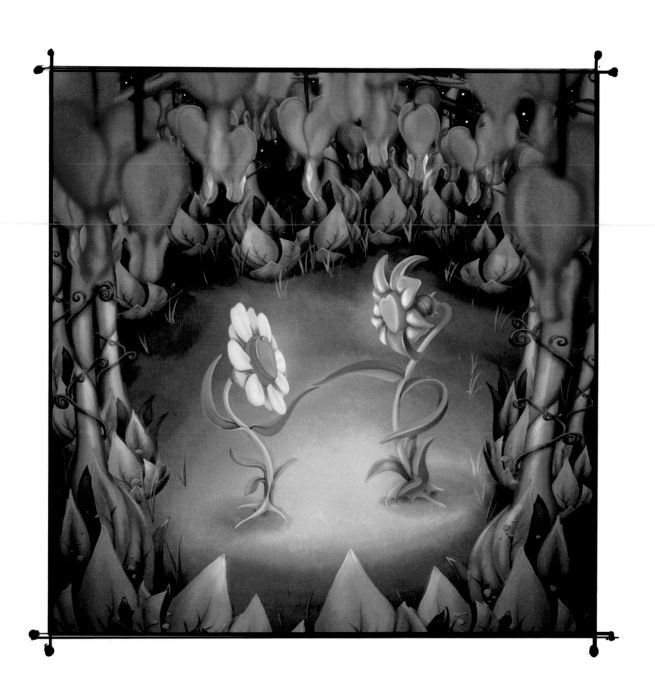

Spread a little kindness
Sprinkle as you go
Send it out into the world
Watch it ebb and flow

Plant a kindness garden
The more seeds that you sow
You'll find that your own happiness
will grow,
and grow,
and grow!

If a shark attacked
I would bump him off track
By the nose
With the book I was reading

Mr. Shark, I would say
Such behavior betrays
You're a product of misguided eating

So I'll thank you to please
Take your teeth from my knees
And go chomp them around
Somewhere else

And perhaps you will find
Food of proper kind
Further down in those
Fifty-foot swells.

Mary Lou Muggins
Would giggle all day
She'd snicker and laugh
And just chuckle away

No matter what anyone
Did or they said
She'd laugh and she'd laugh
Till her face was bright red

Mary Lou Muggins
Thought everything funny
She laughed at her clothing
She laughed at her honey

She laughed and she laughed
Till her tummy was sore
Then she thought to herself
I won't laugh anymore...

Ahh...
What a lovely summer day...

Ahh...
I love the sprinkler spray...

Ahh...
It's the perfect time to play...

Bzzzz...
What's that sound, hey!

BZZZZ!
RUN AWAY! RUN AWAY!

Grab your coats and grab your hats
Pack your smiles and pack your laughs
And don't forget a snack or two
We're travelin' in hot air balloons!

Now hop aboard, we fly today
The cars and houses melt away
Then up, up, up, we'll be there soon
We're sailing straight on to the moon!

Itchy itchy itchy
I'll play connect the dots
With all these itchy itchy
Little itchy pink round spots

Itchy itchy itchy
If they don't say cluck or boc
Then why oh why are these itchy things
Called itchy chickenpox?

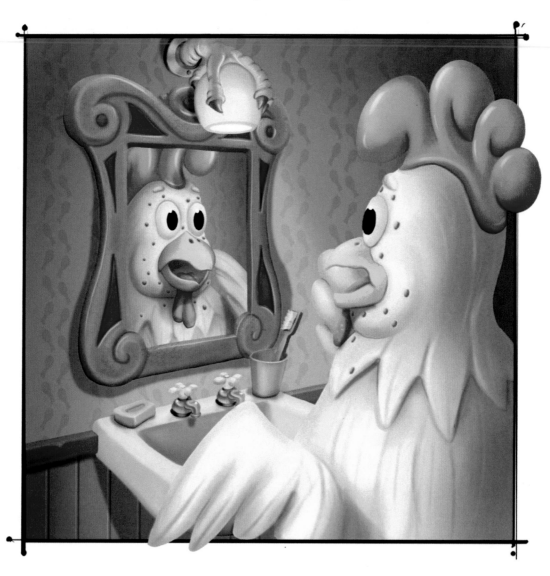

Ring, ring, ring!
Golly, what's that sound?
Ring, ding, ding
I'm looking all around

Bring, bring, bring!
I hear that sound once more!
Ding a ling a ling...

All this looking
Made me tired
And the sound has
Now expired

So I think I'll take a nap here on the floor...

There's a way to travel without travelin'
To see the whole wide world from your bed
Just start thinkin' and a-dreamin' and a-wanderin'
With the stuff that's in your heart and in your head

Now that stuff isn't a something you grab hold of
Well, at least not with a net or with your hands
And exactly what it is or where it comes from
Isn't something that you'll always understand

But that something has a name, and it's called magic
Or imagination, if you like that more
And if you're packed and ready for adventure
Well,
That's precisely what that something's waiting for

Now come on, hurry up, let's go explore!

Jingle jingle, little gnome
Have you found your way back home?
Marching through the woods all day
I sure hope you've found your way

Jingle jingle, little friend
Now the day has reached its end
Up above the bright moon beams
Close your eyes and sleep sweet dreams!

At the end of the evening
If you've done your best
Then smile a big smile
And be happy and rest
And if you start thinking
You could have done more
Keep smiling,
'Cause that's what tomorrow is for.

The End
(Until next time...)

Use your imagination
For magical creation
An artsy celebration
Brought forth by this decree ~

There are no rules
To creativity!

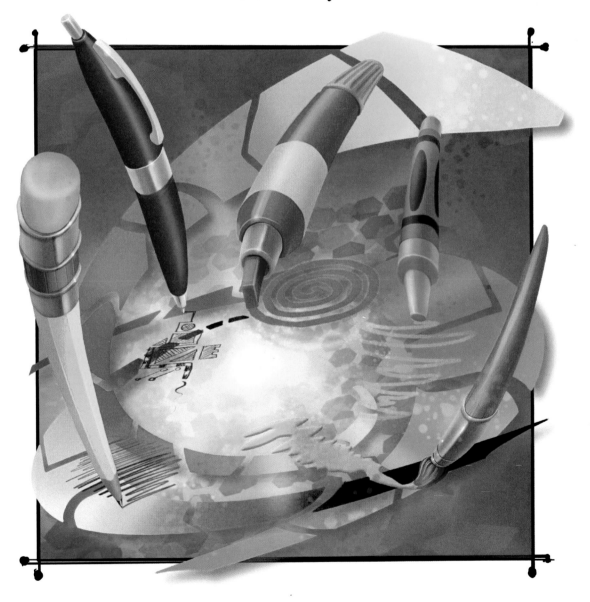

For more books and fun visit
www.laurajaworski.com

Visit the illustrator at
gjmeyer.wix.com/portfolio

Made in the USA
Middletown, DE
07 March 2021